You're in such good hands. I pray you sense the nearness of God's loving presence.

*Come near to God,
and God will come near to you.*

JAMES 4:8 NCV

If you ever feel that no one can help you, hear you, or heed your call, you aren't alone. I don't mean you aren't alone in knowing the feeling. I mean you aren't alone. Period.

Max Lucado

DaySpring

WHERE YOU ARE WEAK, GOD IS MORE THAN STRONG ENOUGH. I'M ASKING HIM TO GIVE YOU HIS STRENGTH IN AMAZING WAYS TODAY.

I can do all things through Christ, because He gives me strength.

PHILIPPIANS 4:13 NCV

You are never without help, hope, or strength. You are stronger than you think because God is nearer than you might imagine.

MAX LUCADO

DaySpring

I'm praying that you feel God's tenderness toward you today.

The LORD is like a father to His children,
tender and compassionate
to those who fear Him.

PSALM 103:13 NLT

You have a God who hears you,
the power of love behind you,
the Holy Spirit within you,
and all of heaven ahead of you.

Max Lucado

DaySpring

GOOD NEWS: THERE'S REALLY NO SUCH THING AS IMPOSSIBLE FOR YOU, BECAUSE ALL THINGS ARE POSSIBLE WITH GOD. PRAYING YOU KNOW THE REALITY OF THAT TODAY!

Jesus looked at them and said,
"With man this is impossible,
but not with God;
all things are possible with God."

MARK 10:27 NIV

When we believe, we find strength beyond our strength.

MAX LUCADO

DaySpring

The world doesn't rest on your shoulders—even when it feels like it does. I'm praying you will have the faith to see the One who is ready and willing to help you in all things.

I tell you the truth, if your faith is as big as a mustard seed, you can say to this mountain, "Move from here to there," and it will move. All things will be possible for you.

MATTHEW 17:20 NCV

When we believe, we accomplish tasks beyond our capacity.

Max Lucado

DaySpring

I'M PRAYING GOD GIVES YOU THE WISDOM YOU NEED TO MAKE THE HARD DECISIONS.

If any of you needs wisdom, you should ask God for it. He is generous to everyone and will give you wisdom without criticizing you.

JAMES 1:5 NCV

When we believe, we see solutions beyond our wisdom.

MAX LUCADO

DaySpring

You don't have to do life on your own. Help is available! I'm praying you sense His reassuring comfort today.

The Lord Himself will go before you.
He will be with you; He will not leave you or forget you. Don't be afraid and don't worry.

DEUTERONOMY 31:8–9 NCV

Meet today's problems with today's strength.
Don't start tackling tomorrow's problems until tomorrow.
You do not have tomorrow's strength yet.
You simply have enough for today.

Max Lucado

DaySpring

I'M PRAYING THAT YOU ALWAYS FEEL GOD'S HAND IN YOURS AS YOU WALK THE ROAD OF LIFE.

Don't worry, because I am with you.
Don't be afraid, because I am your God.
I will make you strong and will help you;
I will support you with My right hand
that saves you.

ISAIAH 41:10 NCV

Belief is a decision to lean entirely upon the strength of a living and loving Savior.

MAX LUCADO

DaySpring

I'm praying that as God directs your steps, you will feel secure in the knowledge that He'll lead you into all the right places.

I am with you always, to the end of the age.

MATTHEW 28:20 ESV

You and I are never, ever alone.
Was this not one of the final promises of Christ?

Max Lucado

DaySpring

EVEN WHEN OTHER PEOPLE LET YOU DOWN, GOD IS ALWAYS THERE TO LOVE YOU AND HELP YOU ALONG THE WAY. PRAYING YOU FEEL HIS CLOSE PRESENCE TODAY.

Trust the LORD always,
because He is our Rock forever.

ISAIAH 26:4 NCV

Lift your eyes and open your heart to the possibility—indeed, the reality—that the greatest force in the universe is One who means you well and brings you hope.

MAX LUCADO

DaySpring

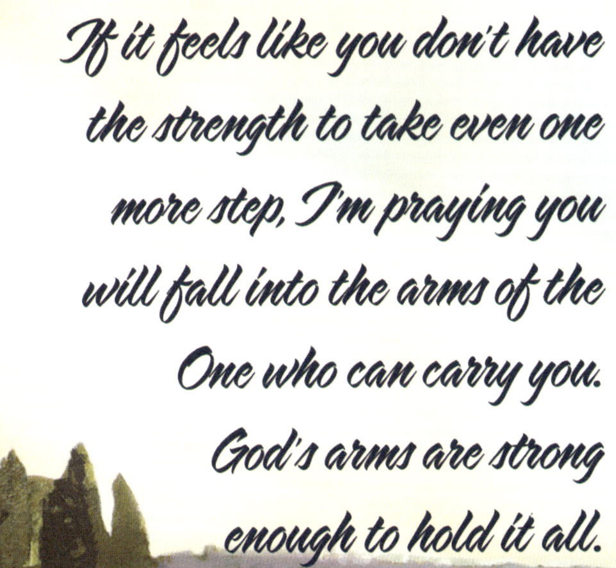

If it feels like you don't have the strength to take even one more step, I'm praying you will fall into the arms of the One who can carry you. God's arms are strong enough to hold it all.

Even when you are old, I will be the same. Even when your hair has turned gray, I will take care of you. I made you and will take care of you. I will carry you and save you.

ISAIAH 46:4 NCV

God's got this! Think it's up to you and you ain't much? Hogwash. God can carry you.

Max Lucado

DaySpring

TODAY, I PRAY THAT A SILENT MOMENT OR TWO WON'T BE HARD TO COME BY. THAT YOU'LL ENJOY PEACE IN GOD'S PRESENCE AND REST FOR YOUR SOUL.

The Lord is with you when you are with Him.

II CHRONICLES 15:2 NCV

You're stronger than you think
because God is nearer than you know.

MAX LUCADO

DaySpring

When things are dark and the way forward is uncertain, I'm asking the Lord to make His nearness known to you.

Lord, tell me Your ways. Show me how to live. Guide me in Your truth, and teach me, my God, my Savior. I trust You all day long.

PSALM 25:4-5 NCV

There was a message in the miracles of Jesus: "I am here. I care."

Max Lucado

DaySpring

I KNOW GOD UNDERSTANDS YOUR SITUATION. AND I'M ASKING HIM TO BLESS YOU WITH MORE THAN YOU COULD EVER ASK OR IMAGINE.

He is the One you should praise;
He is Your God, who has done great and wonderful things for you,
which you have seen with your own eyes.

DEUTERONOMY 10:21 NCV

Jesus wants us to understand that there is a miracle-working God who loves, cares, and comes to our aid.

MAX LUCADO

DaySpring

God says that when we ask for wisdom, He will give it. I will pray, today and every day, for exactly the wisdom you need.

Those who know the LORD *trust Him, because He will not leave those who come to Him.*

PSALM 9:10 NCV

We can set our weight fully upon the strength of our loving God.

Max Lucado

DaySpring

ONLY THE LORD KNOWS EXACTLY WHAT YOU NEED FOR FULL RESTORATION . . . AND HE CAN DO IT. I'M PRAYING FOR YOU.

"I will bring back your health and heal your injuries," says the LORD.

JEREMIAH 30:17 NCV

God will replenish what life has taken.

MAX LUCADO

DaySpring

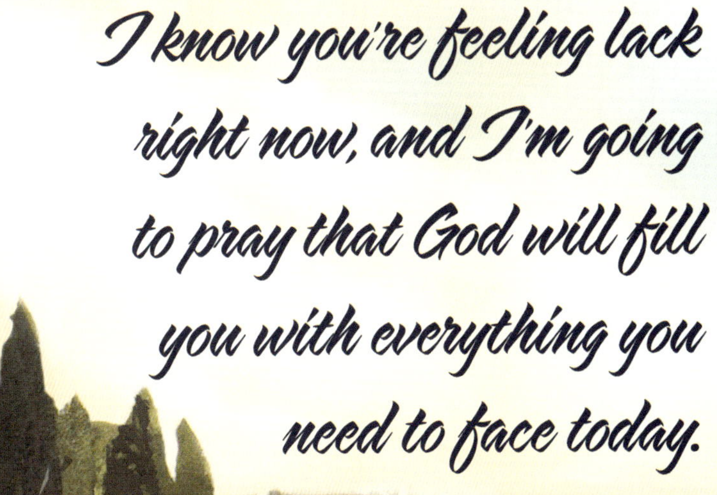

I know you're feeling lack right now, and I'm going to pray that God will fill you with everything you need to face today.

God can give you more blessings than you need. Then you will always have plenty of everything— enough to give to every good work.

II CORINTHIANS 9:8 NCV

Our diminishing supplies,
no matter how insignificant,
matter to heaven.

Max Lucado

DaySpring

GOD CARES, AND I'M PRAYING HE SHOWS YOU JUST HOW MUCH HE CARES TODAY.

God is our protection and our strength.
He always helps in times of trouble.

Psalm 46:1 NCV

We are under the care of God's ever-present help.

MAX LUCADO

DaySpring

It's not unusual to feel alone in challenging times. I'm praying that you know without a doubt that God is beside you.

Be strong and courageous!
Do not be afraid and do not panic before them.
For the LORD your God will personally go ahead of you. He will neither fail you nor abandon you.

DEUTERONOMY 31:6 NLT

Though the storm was severe, my Lord was near.
And I learned a lesson I've never forgotten:
Jesus comes in the midst of the torrent.

Max Lucado

DaySpring

HE'S A GOOD, GOOD FATHER. I'M PRAYING THAT GOD SHOWS YOU JUST HOW MUCH HE CARES.

If your children ask for a fish,
would you give them a snake? . . .
You know how to give good gifts to
your children. How much more
your heavenly Father will give
good things to those who ask Him!

MATTHEW 7:10–11 NCV

It falls to the father to heed the need and respond to the request of the child.

MAX LUCADO

DaySpring

I believe that not only does God care, but He has the perfect solution to your need. That's the confidence I'm praying with today.

Seek first God's kingdom
and what God wants.
Then all your other needs
will be met as well.

MATTHEW 6:33 NCV

Have you turned your deficit into a prayer? Jesus will tailor a response to your precise need.

Max Lucado

DaySpring

EVEN WHEN YOU FEEL UNSEEN OR OVERLOOKED, GOD IS MINDFUL OF YOU. I'M BELIEVING ALL THE GOOD THAT GOD HAS IN STORE.

Whatever is good and perfect is a gift coming down to us from God our Father.

JAMES 1:17 NLT

God is not a fast-food cook. He is an accomplished chef who prepares unique blessings for unique situations.

MAX LUCADO

DaySpring

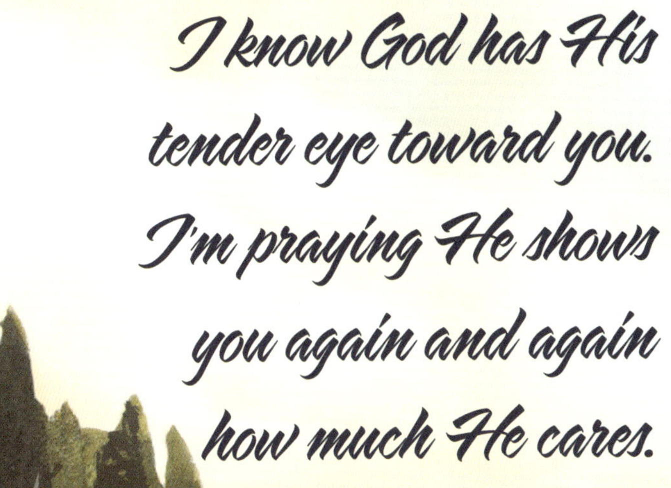

I know God has His tender eye toward you. I'm praying He shows you again and again how much He cares.

Your Father knows the things you need before you ask Him.

MATTHEW 6:8 NCV

Our prayers may be awkward. Our attempts may be feeble. But since the power of prayer is in the one who hears it and not in the one who says it, our prayers do make a difference.

Max Lucado

WHEN WE PRAY, WE CAN TRUST THAT GOD'S OUTCOME IS THE BEST ONE. I'M ASKING HIM TO LEAD YOU CLEARLY!

*The LORD says, "I will guide you
along the best pathway for your life.
I will advise you and watch over you."*

Psalm 32:8 NLT

Jesus is in charge. I'm not.

MAX LUCADO

I know that God's plans for you are so good. I'm asking Him to accomplish them quickly on your behalf.

God can do much, much more than anything we can ask or imagine.

EPHESIANS 3:20 NCV

Something powerful happens when we present our needs to Jesus and trust Him to do what is right: He is able to do exceedingly more than we would ever think.

Max Lucado

DaySpring

HOLD ON TIGHT AND BELIEVE THIS: YOU'RE DOING GREAT. I'M PRAYING FOR YOU!

We know that in everything God works for the good of those who love Him.

ROMANS 8:28 NCV

Be patient. God is using today's difficulties to strengthen you for tomorrow.

MAX LUCADO

DaySpring

I'm praying you'll have the faith needed to take the next step forward.

Without faith no one can please God. Anyone who comes to God must believe that He is real and that He rewards those who truly want to find Him.

HEBREWS 11:6 NCV

Feed your fears, and your faith will starve. Feed your faith, and your fears will.

Max Lucado

DaySpring

I'M PRAYING YOU SENSE GOD'S LOVING PRESENCE TODAY. I KNOW HE'S WITH YOU EVERY STEP OF THE WAY.

Never will I leave you;
never will I forsake you.

HEBREWS 13:5 NIV

Read the Bible from the table of contents in the front to the maps in the back, and you will not find any promise of a pain-free life on this side of death. But you will find the assurance of His presence.

MAX LUCADO

DaySpring

Praying you feel God's presence and guidance every moment.

The LORD will guide you continually, giving you water when you are dry and restoring your strength.

ISAIAH 58:11 NLT

God is ever-present. Not occasional or sporadic. You'll never be put on hold or told to check back later.

Max Lucado

DaySpring

PRAYING YOU'LL SENSE GOD'S LOVE IN A SPECIAL WAY AND KNOW HE'S CLOSE BY YOUR SIDE . . . TODAY AND ALWAYS.

Where can I go from Your Spirit?
Where can I flee from Your presence?
If I go up to the heavens, You are there;
if I make my bed in the depths, You are there.

PSALM 139:7–8 NIV

God is ever-present. As near as your next breath. Closer than your own skin.

MAX LUCADO

DaySpring

No one knows what the future holds. But I know who holds us. Praying that God will work everything out amazingly for you.

I will be your God throughout your lifetime—
until your hair is white with age.
I made you, and I will care for you.
I will carry you along and save you.

ISAIAH 46:4 NLT

Assume that something good is going to happen.

Max Lucado

DaySpring

I'M THINKING OF YOU TODAY—PRAYING THAT EVERY MOMENT IS FILLED WITH GOD'S BLESSINGS FOR YOU.

God began doing a good work in you, and I am sure He will continue it until it is finished when Jesus Christ comes again.

PHILIPPIANS 1:6 NCV

The Divine Artist isn't finished yet.
The earth is His studio.
Every person on earth is one of His projects.
Every event on earth is part of God's great mural.

MAX LUCADO

DaySpring

Wherever you feel afraid today, I'm praying that God will meet you there and remind you of His love and care.

I will not be afraid,
because the LORD is with me.

PSALM 118:6 NCV

The presence of fear does not mean you have no faith. Fear visits everyone. But make your fear a visitor and not a resident.

Max Lucado

DaySpring

I'M PRAYING YOU'LL SEE GOD'S GUIDANCE AND CARE FOR YOU TODAY.

*Your word is like a lamp for
my feet and a light for my path.*

PSALM 119:105 NCV

Jesus has spoken.
Let His Word do what it was intended to do:
lead you home.

MAX LUCADO

DaySpring

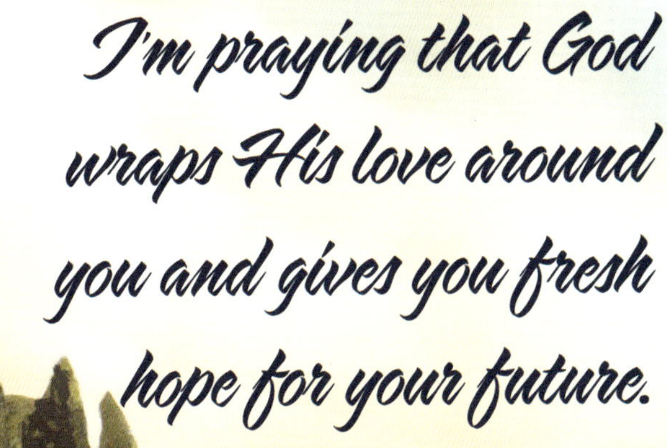

"I know the plans I have for you," declares the Lord, "plans to prosper you and not to harm you, plans to give you hope and a future."

JEREMIAH 29:11 NIV

Heed the invitation of this miracle:
Believe in the Jesus who believes in you.
He believes that you can rise up, take up, and move on.
You are stronger than you think.

Max Lucado

DaySpring

ASKING GOD TO HOLD YOUR HAND TIGHT AND SHOW YOU ALL THE GOOD THINGS HE HAS IN STORE.

People can make all kinds of plans,
but only the LORD's plan will happen.

Proverbs 19:21 NCV

God's help, while ever present, is ever specific.
It is not ours to say what God will do.
Our job is to believe He will do something.

MAX LUCADO

DaySpring

I'm asking God to gently counsel you, constantly reassure you, and lovingly lead you through.

Trust the LORD with all your heart,
and don't depend on your own understanding.
Remember the LORD in all you do,
and He will give you success.

PROVERBS 3:5–6 NCV

God dismantled the neutral gear from your transmission. He is the God of forward motion, the God of tomorrow.

Max Lucado

DaySpring

I'M PRAYING THAT YOU'LL RECEIVE GOD'S ABUNDANT WISDOM WHEN YOU ASK FOR IT. I KNOW THAT GOD HAS THE VERY BEST FOR YOU!

Only the Lord *gives wisdom;*
He gives knowledge and understanding.

Proverbs 2:6 NCV

Ask the Lord this question:
What can I do today that will take me
in the direction of a better tomorrow?
Keep asking until you hear an answer.
And once you hear it, do it.

MAX LUCADO

DaySpring

I am praying for the courage you need to trust the Lord. He will lead you through.

On the day I called to You,
You answered me.
You made me strong and brave.

PSALM 138:3 NCV

What we cannot do, Christ does!

Max Lucado

DaySpring

I'M ASKING GOD TO ILLUMINATE A PATHWAY FOR YOU TO NAVIGATE OUT OF THIS TROUBLESOME SITUATION. AND HE'LL WALK WITH YOU EACH STEP OF THE WAY.

When troubles of any kind come your way,
consider it an opportunity for great joy.
For you know that when your faith is tested,
your endurance has a chance to grow.

JAMES 1:2–3 NLT

If you see your troubles as opportunities to trust God
and His ability to multiply what you give Him,
then even the smallest incidents take on significance.

MAX LUCADO

DaySpring

I'm praying you discover God's faithfulness time and time again.

Happy is the person who trusts the Lord.

PSALM 40:4 NCV

Count first on Christ.
He can help you do the impossible.

Max Lucado

WHATEVER YOU HAVE TO OFFER TODAY, I'M PRAYING THAT GOD WOULD MULTIPLY IT AND SURPRISE YOU WITH WHAT HE CAN DO WITH WHAT YOU HAVE.

God can do anything, you know—far more than you could ever imagine or guess or request in your wildest dreams!

EPHESIANS 3:20 THE MESSAGE

It's not for you and me to tell Jesus our gift is too small. God can take a small thing and do a big thing.

MAX LUCADO

DaySpring

You are held and loved during this time. I'm praying you feel God's closeness in all that you do.

The life of every creature and the breath of all people are in God's hand.

JOB 12:10 NCV

You aren't alone. You aren't without help. What bewilders you does not bewilder God.

Max Lucado

DaySpring

I'M ASKING THE LORD TO GUIDE YOUR HOPES, DESIRES, AND STEPS TO MATCH HIS VERY BEST FOR YOU. IT WILL ALL WORK OUT, I PROMISE.

People may make plans in their minds,
but the Lord decides what they will do.

PROVERBS 16:9 NCV

Though we may not be able to see His purpose or His plan, the Lord of heaven is on His throne and in firm control of the universe and our lives.

MAX LUCADO

DaySpring

When you feel like the storms of life will take you out, I'm praying you'll see God is right there with you.

In their misery they cried out to the Lord,
and He saved them from their troubles.
He stilled the storm and calmed the waves.

PSALM 107:28–29 NCV

Jesus comes in the midst of the torrent.

Max Lucado

DaySpring

THERE'S NOTHING TO FEAR WHEN GOD IS NEAR. STAY STRONG, AND KNOW THAT I'M PRAYING FOR YOU.

When you go through deep waters,
I will be with you.

ISAIAH 43:2 NLT

Before Jesus stills the storms,
He comes to us in the midst of our storms.
MAX LUCADO

DaySpring

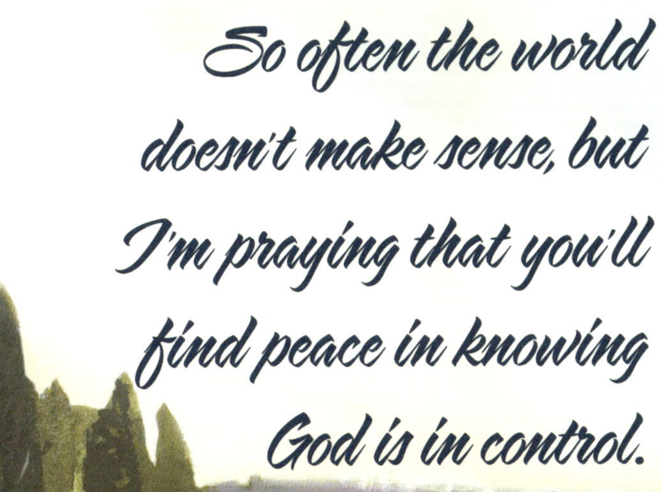

Peace I leave with you. My peace I give to you.
I do not give to you as the world gives.
Don't let your heart be troubled or fearful.

JOHN 14:27 CSB

God is God. He knows what He is doing.
When you can't trace His hand, trust His heart.

Max Lucado

DaySpring

I WANT YOU TO KNOW THAT I'M PRAYING FOR YOU UNTIL YOU SEE A CLEAR PATH FORWARD. I KNOW IT'S COMING!

The Lord makes firm the steps of the
one who delights in Him;
though he may stumble, he will not fall,
for the Lord upholds him with His hand.

Psalm 37:23–24 NIV

When we see nothing but darkness, feel nothing but doubt, and wonder if God is near or aware, the welcome answer from Jesus is this: "I AM."

MAX LUCADO

DaySpring

Never forget that God is with you. I'm praying you see evidence of His closeness in your situation.

Surely God is my help;
the Lord is the one who sustains me.

PSALM 54:4 NIV

Don't try to weather this storm alone.
Row the boat and bail the water,
but above all bid Christ to enter your sinking craft.

Max Lucado

DaySpring

IN YOUR MOMENTS OF FEAR AND DISCOURAGEMENT, I'M PRAYING YOU WILL FEEL GOD'S COMFORTING PRESENCE.

Do not be afraid or discouraged.
For the Lord *your God is*
with you wherever you go.

Joshua 1:9 NLT

Believe that you are never alone,
that our miracle-working God sees you,
cares about you, and will come to your aid.

MAX LUCADO

DaySpring

*When it's hard to wait,
I'm praying God will
give you His amazing
grace and peace.*

*May the Lord lead your
hearts into God's love and
Christ's patience.*

II THESSALONIANS 3:5 NCV

The next time you pray,
"Is anyone coming to help me?"
Listen for the response of Jesus:
"I AM with you in the storm."

Max Lucado

DaySpring

GOD DESIGNED YOU ON PURPOSE AND CARES FOR YOU SPECIFICALLY. I'M ASKING HIM TO BE VERY CLEAR ABOUT HIS LOVE FOR YOU TODAY.

So I tell you, ask,
and God will give to you.
Search, and you will find.
Knock, and the door will open for you.

LUKE 11:9 NCV

God is not a one-size-fits-all Savior.
Perceiving unique needs,
He issues unique blessings.
MAX LUCADO

DaySpring

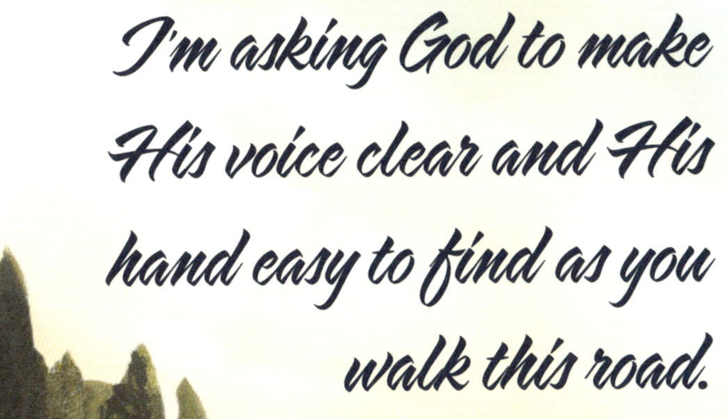

I am the LORD your God,
who holds your right hand,
and I tell you, "Don't be afraid.
I will help you."

ISAIAH 41:13 NCV

It is not God's will that we grope blindly through life.
He will do whatever it takes to help us see how to see.

Max Lucado

DaySpring

I'M PRAYING YOU FIND HOPE VERY SOON.

The reason Christ died and rose from the dead to live again was so He would be Lord over both the dead and the living.

ROMANS 14:9 NCV

Jesus meets us in the cemeteries of life. Whether we are there to say goodbye or there to be buried, we can count on the presence of God.

MAX LUCADO

DaySpring

I know you feel stuck. I'm praying God will open just the right doors for you.

See, I am doing a new thing!
Now it springs up; do you not perceive it?
I am making a way in the wilderness and
streams in the wasteland.

ISAIAH 43:19 NIV

God cast you in His play, wrote you into His story.
He has a definite direction for your life.
Fulfill it and enjoy fulfillment.
Play the part God prepared for you and
get ready for some great days.

Max Lucado

DaySpring

I'M ASKING GOD TO SHOWER YOU WITH AMAZING GRACE TODAY. YOUR LIFE IS IN HIS LOVING HANDS.

God was in Christ,
making peace between
the world and Himself.
In Christ, God did not hold
the world guilty of its sins.

II CORINTHIANS 5:19 NCV

God does not count our sins against us!

MAX LUCADO

DaySpring

Nothing could ever keep God from loving you. I'm praying it's easy for you to believe that today.

You have been saved
by grace through believing.
You did not save yourselves;
it was a gift from God.

EPHESIANS 2:8 NCV

Let the grace of God flow over you
like a cleansing cascade,
flushing out all dregs of guilt and shame.

Max Lucado

DaySpring

I'M ASKING GOD TO RELIEVE YOUR WORRIES AND GIVE YOU HIS STRENGTH FOR TODAY.

Cast your cares on the LORD *and He will sustain you.*

PSALM 55:22 NIV

Worry is irrelevant. It alters nothing. When was the last time you solved a problem by worrying about it?

MAX LUCADO

DaySpring

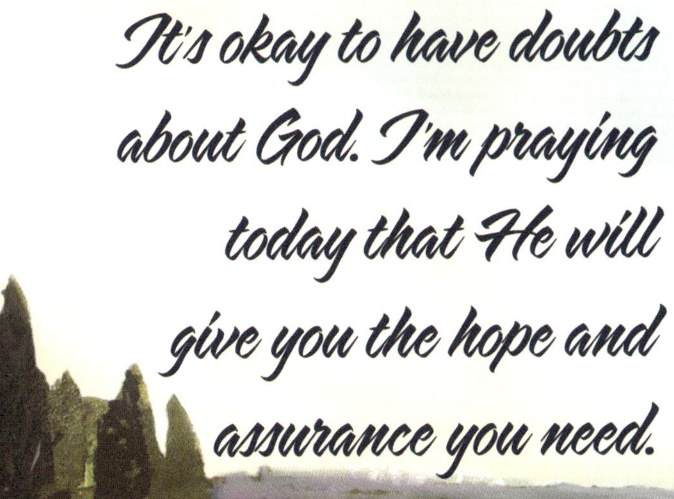

It's okay to have doubts about God. I'm praying today that He will give you the hope and assurance you need.

"I do believe;
help me overcome my unbelief!"

MARK 9:24 NIV

Faith is not the absence of doubt. Faith is simply a willingness to keep asking the hard questions.

Max Lucado

DaySpring

I'M PRAYING GOD WILL REVEAL HIS LOVE FOR YOU IN AN AMAZING WAY TODAY.

As high as the sky
is above the earth,
so great is His love for those
who respect Him.

PSALM 103:11 NCV

Trust God's love. His perfect love . . .
With perfect knowledge of the past and
perfect vision of the future,
He loves you perfectly in spite of both.

MAX LUCADO

DaySpring

You are such a beautiful work in progress. I'm asking God to help you know that for certain.

God began doing a good work in you, and I am sure He will continue it until it is finished when Jesus Christ comes again.

PHILIPPIANS 1:6 NCV

Christ is not finished with you.
You might be down, but you are not out.

Max Lucado

DaySpring

THERE'S NOTHING OUT OF GOD'S REACH, INCLUDING YOU. I'M PRAYING YOU FEEL HIS PEACEFUL PRESENCE.

Those who go to God Most High for safety
will be protected by the Almighty.

PSALM 91:1 NCV

God sends His angels to protect us and
His Word as a star to guide us.
Then He surrounds us with His grace.

MAX LUCADO

DaySpring

I'm praying you know how truly treasured you are by God. You are a gift to the world.

We are God's handiwork,
created in Christ Jesus to do good works,
which God prepared in advance for us to do.

EPHESIANS 2:10 NIV

God sees in you a masterpiece about to happen.

Max Lucado

DaySpring

I'M PRAYING FOR YOU, FRIEND. LET'S BE AMAZED TOGETHER AT WHAT GOD CAN DO.

God can pour on the blessings in astonishing ways so that you're ready for anything and everything, more than just ready to do what needs to be done.

II CORINTHIANS 9:8 THE MESSAGE

Why would Jesus walk on water, feed thousands, and raise the dead? So that you would believe God still stills the storms of life, still solves the problems of life, and still brings dead things to life.

MAX LUCADO

DaySpring

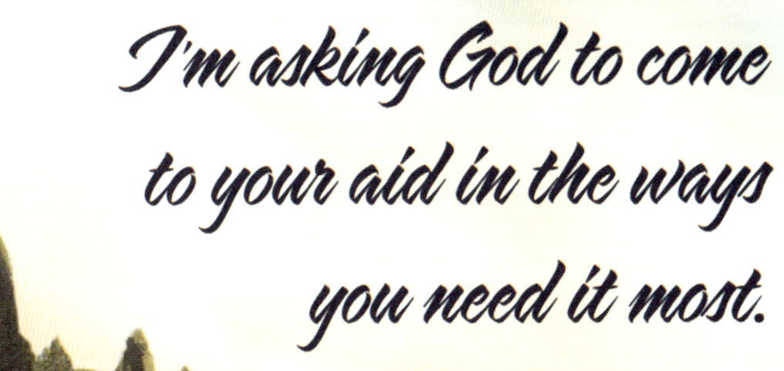

Is anyone crying for help?
God is listening, ready to rescue you.

PSALM 34:17 THE MESSAGE

The miracle-working God cares for you, fights for you, and will come to your aid.

Max Lucado

DaySpring

I CAN'T WAIT TO SEE HOW YOU COME THROUGH THIS. I'LL BE PRAYING THE WHOLE TIME.

If God is for us, who can ever be against us?

Romans 8:31 NLT

God wants us to win in faith, hope, and life.
He marshals every force, enlists every tool,
employs every miracle so you and I will
someday throw triumphant fists into the sky.

MAX LUCADO

DaySpring

You are an amazing human with an amazing future. I'm praying for God to accomplish all He wants to through you.

Let us hold firmly to the hope that we have confessed, because we can trust God to do what He promised.

HEBREWS 10:23 NCV

We are not weathervanes whipped about by the winds of fate and chance. We are the children of a mighty and good God who cares for us.

Max Lucado

DaySpring

I PRAY YOU KNOW HOW SPECIAL YOU ARE TO GOD. HOW NEEDED YOU ARE IN THIS WORLD.

We are God's masterpiece.
He has created us anew in Christ Jesus,
so we can do the good things
He planned for us long ago.

Ephesians 2:10 NLT

You are stronger than you think because God is nearer than you might imagine.

MAX LUCADO

DaySpring

I'm asking God to reveal His presence to you today, and to remind you that He is in control and that His love and care for you are unwavering.

Don't worry, because I am with you.
Don't be afraid, because I am your God.
I will make you strong and will help you;
I will support you with My right hand
that saves you.

ISAIAH 41:10 NCV

God never said that the journey would be easy,
but He did say that the arrival would be worthwhile.

Max Lucado

DaySpring

I'M PRAYING FOR YOU, FRIEND. I BELIEVE GOD HAS GREAT THINGS IN STORE FOR YOU.

I go to bed and sleep in peace, because, Lord, only You keep me safe.

PSALM 4:8 NCV

May you believe that God is your ever-present help. And in His presence may you find rest.

MAX LUCADO

DaySpring

I'm asking God to bless you!

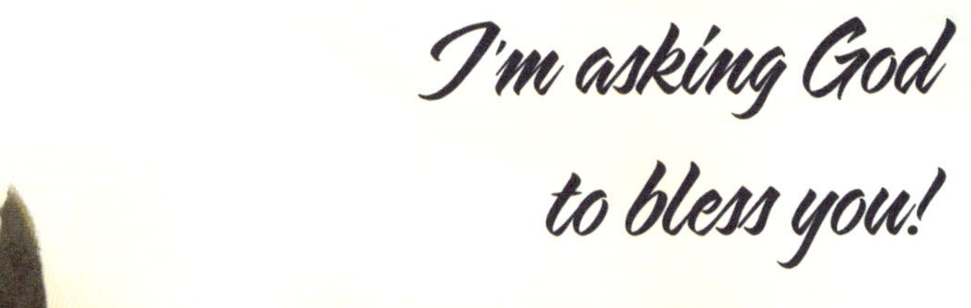

May the Lord bless you and keep you.
May the Lord show you His kindness
and have mercy on you.
May the Lord watch over you
and give you peace.

NUMBERS 6:24–26 NCV

God's blessings are dispensed according to the riches of His grace, not according to the depth of our faith.

Max Lucado

DaySpring

NO MATTER WHAT YOU'VE DONE OR WHERE YOU'VE BEEN, GOD LOVES YOU. I'M PRAYING YOU'LL FEEL HIS GREAT LOVE TODAY.

Nothing above us, nothing below us, nor anything else in the whole world will ever be able to separate us from the love of God that is in Christ Jesus our Lord.

ROMANS 8:39 NCV

Nothing separates you from God.

MAX LUCADO

DaySpring

It's not always easy to trust the process, but I'm praying that you'll have all the patience and grace you need as you wait on the Lord.

I pray that the God who gives hope will fill you with much joy and peace while you trust in Him. Then your hope will overflow by the power of the Holy Spirit.

ROMANS 15:13 NCV

When we wonder if God is coming,
He answers with His name: "I AM!"

Max Lucado

I'M PRAYING YOUR HEART WILL BE ENCOURAGED THIS WEEK AND GOD WILL GIVE YOU FRESH HOPE.

Anyone who belongs to Christ
has become a new person.
The old life is gone; a new life has begun!

II Corinthians 5:17 NLT

Rather than ask God to change your circumstances, ask Him to use your circumstances to change you.

MAX LUCADO

DaySpring

I'm asking God to fill your heart with peace and joy during this difficult time.

Depend on the Lord; trust Him,
and He will take care of you.
Then your goodness will shine like the sun,
and your fairness like the noonday sun.

PSALM 37:5–6 NCV

When you trust God, the challenges you face become a canvas upon which He can demonstrate His finest work.

Max Lucado

DaySpring

WHATEVER YOU NEED MOST TODAY, I KNOW GOD CAN DO IT. I'M PRAYING ALONGSIDE YOU.

Be anxious for nothing, but in everything by prayer and supplication, with thanksgiving, let your requests be made known to God.

PHILIPPIANS 4:6 NKJV

You can take your needs—all your needs—to God.

MAX LUCADO

DaySpring

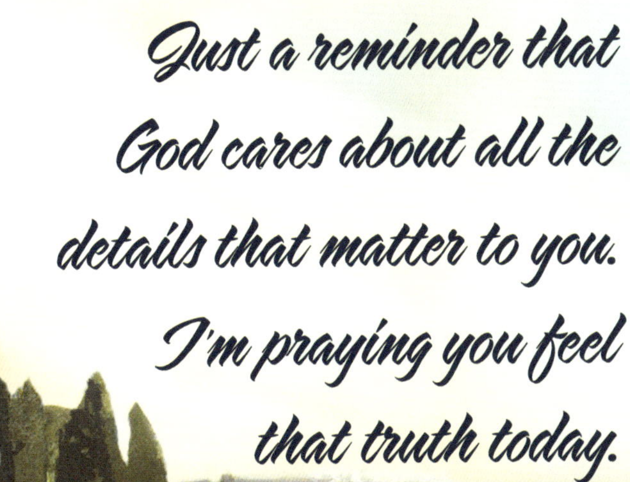

Just a reminder that God cares about all the details that matter to you. I'm praying you feel that truth today.

Two sparrows cost only a penny, but not even one of them can die without your Father's knowing it . . . So don't be afraid. You are worth much more than many sparrows.

MATTHEW 10:29, 31 NCV

In everything—not just the big things—let your requests be made known to God.

Max Lucado

DaySpring

NO MATTER WHAT YOU NEED, YOU CAN TELL GOD. I'M PRAYING YOU WILL SEE HIS CARE AND THE WAY THAT HE PROVIDES FOR YOU TODAY.

Always be joyful.
Pray continually, and give thanks
whatever happens.
That is what God wants
for you in Christ Jesus.

I THESSALONIANS 5:16–18 NCV

Have you turned your deficit into a prayer?
Jesus will tailor a response to your precise need.

MAX LUCADO

DaySpring

When life is confusing and all your plans are crumbling, I'm praying you have a deep peace, knowing that God loves and cares for you.

For as the sky soars high above earth,
so the way I work surpasses
the way you work, and the way
I think is beyond the way you think.

ISAIAH 55:9 THE MESSAGE

God is God. He knows what He is doing.
When you can't trace His hand, trust His heart.

Max Lucado

DaySpring

YOU DON'T HAVE TO FIGURE OUT LIFE ON YOUR OWN. I'M PRAYING GOD WILL GIVE YOU ALL THE WISDOM YOU NEED.

If any of you needs wisdom, you should ask God for it. He is generous to everyone and will give you wisdom without criticizing you.

James 1:5 NCV

Offer a simple prayer and entrust the problem to Christ. Your problem becomes His pathway.

MAX LUCADO

DaySpring

I'm asking God to make His plan clear to you today. It's not always easy to know what to do, but He always knows and can tell you.

Trust God from the bottom of your heart; don't try to figure out everything on your own. Listen for God's voice in everything you do, everywhere you go; He's the one who will keep you on track.

PROVERBS 3:5–6 THE MESSAGE

Whatever God says, whatever He commands, even if His "whatever" is a nothing whatsoever, do it.

Max Lucado

DaySpring

FRIEND, I KNOW THAT WAITING IS TOUGH. I'M ASKING GOD TO GIVE YOU HIS PEACE AND THE ASSURANCE OF HIS CLOSENESS WHILE YOU WAIT.

Be joyful because you have hope.
Be patient when trouble comes,
and pray at all times.

ROMANS 12:12 NCV

Jesus knows what He is doing.

MAX LUCADO

DaySpring

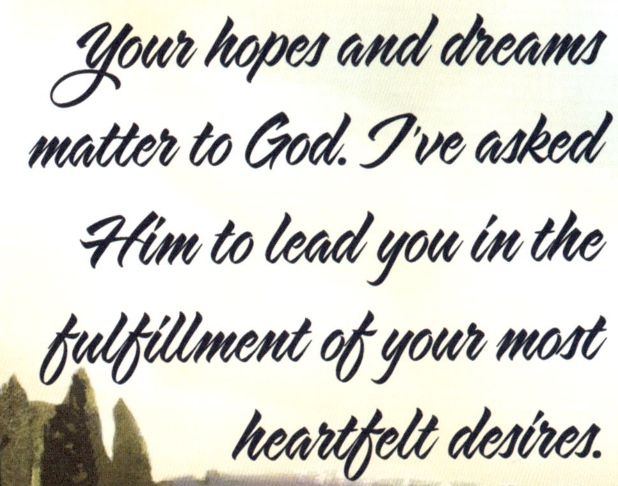

Your hopes and dreams matter to God. I've asked Him to lead you in the fulfillment of your most heartfelt desires.

Praise God, who did not ignore my prayer or hold back His love from me.

PSALM 66:20 NCV

Make your specific request, and trust Him to do not what you want but what is best. Before you know it, you'll be raising a toast in honor of the One who hears your requests.

Max Lucado

DaySpring

AS YOU STEP OUT IN FAITH, GOD WILL STEP IN TO WALK ALONGSIDE YOU, ENCOURAGE YOU, AND STRENGTHEN YOU FOR THE JOURNEY. PRAYING FOR YOU!

Even if I walk through a very dark valley,
I will not be afraid, because You are with me.

PSALM 23:4 NCV

Christ will not remove all the pain this side of heaven. But He will also never leave you alone.

MAX LUCADO

DaySpring

I'm praying that God's nearness is never a question for you. May you always know that He is on your side.

I will never leave you;
I will never abandon you.

HEBREWS 13:5 NCV

God's help is not sporadic.
You'll never be put on hold or told
to check back later.
He's never too busy, preoccupied,
or away on a prior engagement.

Max Lucado

GOD PROMISES NEVER TO LEAVE YOU. I'M PRAYING YOU FEEL HIS PEACEFUL PRESENCE EVERY MOMENT OF EVERY DAY.

The LORD is my rock, my protection,
my Savior. My God is my rock.
I can run to Him for safety.
He is my shield and my saving strength,
my defender.

PSALM 18:2 NCV

God is as near as your next breath.
Closer than your own skin.

MAX LUCADO

DaySpring

God loves you so much and will walk with you through it all. I'm praying for you.

He is not far from any one of us.

ACTS 17:27 NIV

Rehab clinic? He is there. Prison cell? He is present. No boardroom is too superior. No brothel is too vulgar. No palace is too royal. No hovel is too common. He is present.

Max Lucado

DaySpring

I'M PRAYING THAT INSTEAD OF CHOOSING FEAR, YOU CAN LEAN INTO GOD'S TENDERNESS AND TRUST HIM. IT WILL ALL BE OKAY.

We can be sure when we say,
"I will not be afraid, because
the Lord is my helper.
People can't do anything to me."

HEBREWS 13:6 NCV

God is not here to hurt, harm, or hinder.
He is here to help.
MAX LUCADO

DaySpring

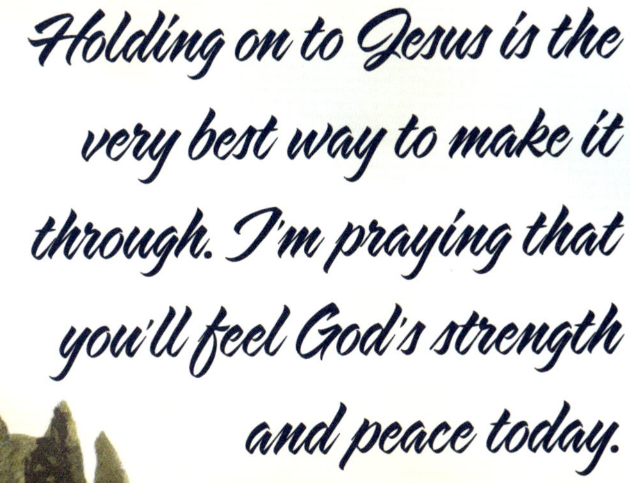

I look up to the hills,
but where does my help come from?
My help comes from the LORD,
who made heaven and earth.

PSALM 121:1–2 NCV

Hang on! Hold on! Don't give up. Help is here. It may not come in the manner you requested or as quickly as you desire, but it will come.

Max Lucado

DaySpring

TODAY, I'M LIFTING YOU UP AND ASKING GOD TO BRING CLARITY TO YOUR SITUATION.

Pray in the Spirit at all times with all kinds of prayers, asking for everything you need. To do this you must always be ready and never give up.

EPHESIANS 6:18 NCV

This life contains many journeys between prayer offered and prayer answered. Jesus promises a blessing at the end of the path.

MAX LUCADO

DaySpring

No matter what you're going through, you're not alone. I'm praying that you feel connected to God and cared for along the way.

I waited patiently for the LORD.
He turned to me and heard my cry.
He lifted me out of the pit of destruction,
out of the sticky mud.

PSALM 40:1–2 NCV

Getting unstuck means getting excited about getting out.

Max Lucado

DaySpring

I'M ASKING GOD TO SHOW YOU HOW MUCH HE BELIEVES IN YOU. YOU WILL MAKE IT THROUGH!

Anyone who comes to God
must believe that He is real
and that He rewards those
who truly want to find Him.

HEBREWS 11:6 NCV

Jesus offers you an invitation:
Believe in the One who believes in you.

MAX LUCADO

DaySpring

I'm asking God to fill you with hope today. You're doing great!

Look at the new thing I am going to do.
It is already happening.
Don't you see it?
I will make a road in the desert
and rivers in the dry land.

ISAIAH 43:19 NCV

What will God do for you?
I cannot say.
Those who claim they can predict
the miracle are less than honest.
But He will certainly resurrect your hope.

Max Lucado

DaySpring

IF YOU ARE IN A HARD CHAPTER, YOU CAN TRUST THAT YOUR STORY ISN'T OVER. PRAYING YOU FEEL GOD'S PEACE AND COMFORT TODAY.

"For I know the plans I have for you," says the Lord. "They are plans for good and not for disaster, to give you a future and a hope."

JEREMIAH 29:11 NLT

God is the God of tomorrow.
He is ready to write a new chapter in your biography.
MAX LUCADO

DaySpring

With God, nothing is impossible. I believe in you—and I'm praying for you too!

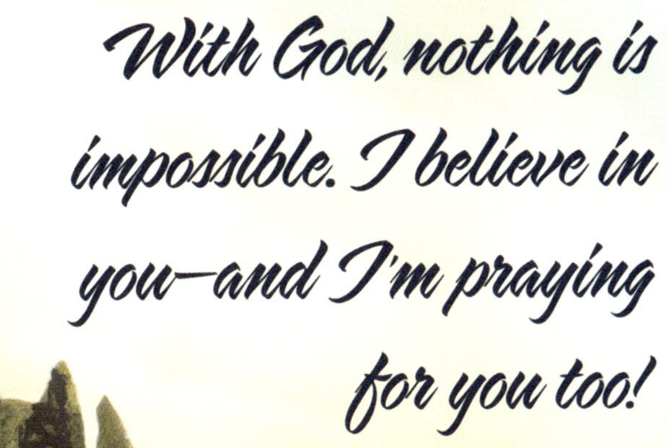

You, Lord, give true peace to those who depend on You.

ISAIAH 26:3 NCV

The problems we face are opportunities for Christ to prove that He does whatever we can't.

Max Lucado

DaySpring

GOD LOVES YOU,
AND HE CARES ABOUT
EVERY STEP YOU TAKE.
SO DO I—
WHICH IS WHY I'M
PRAYING FOR YOU OFTEN!

I'll be with you as you do this, day after day after day, right up to the end of the age.

MATTHEW 28:20 THE MESSAGE

God is always near us. Always for us. Always in us. We may forget Him, but God will never forget us.

MAX LUCADO

DaySpring

Whatever you can offer is enough for God to use. I'm praying for you!

*If you are faithful in little things,
you will be faithful in large ones.*

LUKE 16:10 NLT

All you have is a wimpy prayer?
Give it. All you have is a meager skill? Use it.
All you have is an apology? Offer it.
All you have is strength for one step? Take it.
It's not for you and me to tell Jesus our gift is too small.

Max Lucado

DaySpring

GOD HAS EQUIPPED YOU WITH ALL THAT YOU NEED FOR THIS SEASON. I'M PRAYING YOU FIND THE COURAGE TO STEP FORWARD IN FAITH!

Each of you has received a gift to use to serve others. Be good servants of God's various gifts of grace.

I Peter 4:10 NCV

The people who make a difference are not the ones with the credentials but the ones with the concern.

MAX LUCADO

DaySpring

I'm so thankful nothing is too hard for God. I'm praying His unshakable, unchanging hope fills you with joy today.

Jesus looked at them and said, "For people this is impossible, but for God all things are possible."

MATTHEW 19:26 NCV

Your uphill is downhill for God.
He is not stumped by your problem.

Max Lucado

DaySpring

I'M ASKING GOD TO GIVE YOU HIS STRENGTH AND HELP YOU KNOW HOW DEEPLY YOU ARE LOVED.

Depend on the LORD and His strength;
always go to Him for help.

PSALM 105:4 NCV

Welcome Jesus into the midst
of this turbulent time.
Don't let the storm turn you inward.
Let it turn you upward.

MAX LUCADO

DaySpring